50 Brazilian Feast Recipes for Home

By: Kelly Johnson

Table of Contents

- Feijoada (Brazilian Black Bean Stew)
- Pão de Queijo (Cheese Bread)
- Coxinha (Chicken Croquettes)
- Moqueca de Peixe (Brazilian Fish Stew)
- Brigadeiro (Chocolate Truffles)
- Churrasco (Brazilian BBQ)
- Farofa (Toasted Cassava Flour)
- Caipirinha (Brazilian Cocktail)
- Bobó de Camarão (Shrimp in Cassava Cream)
- Acarajé (Black-Eyed Pea Fritters)
- Vatapá (Spicy Shrimp and Fish Stew)
- Quindim (Coconut Custard)
- Arroz de Carreteiro (Brazilian Beef and Rice)
- Pastel (Brazilian Pastries)
- Beijinho (Coconut Truffles)
- Escondidinho de Carne Seca (Cassava and Jerky Casserole)
- Cocada (Coconut Candy)
- Caldo Verde (Brazilian Green Soup)
- Canjica (Brazilian Sweet Corn Pudding)
- Empadão (Brazilian Meat Pie)
- Pé-de-Moleque (Peanut Brittle)
- Salpicão (Brazilian Chicken Salad)
- Baião de Dois (Rice and Black-Eyed Peas)
- Maria-mole (Coconut Marshmallows)
- Angu (Brazilian Polenta)
- Bolinho de Bacalhau (Codfish Balls)
- Manjar Branco (Coconut Pudding)
- Bolo de Fubá (Cornmeal Cake)
- Cuscuz Paulista (Savory Cornmeal Pudding)
- Mungunzá (Brazilian Corn and Coconut Pudding)
- Carne de Sol (Sun-Dried Beef)
- Sopa Leão Veloso (Brazilian Chicken Soup)
- Canjica Nordestina (Northeastern Brazilian Corn Pudding)
- Arroz Doce (Brazilian Rice Pudding)
- Bauru (Brazilian Sandwich)

- Galinhada (Brazilian Chicken and Rice)
- Casquinha de Siri (Stuffed Crab Shells)
- Pastel de Nata (Portuguese Custard Tart)
- Sorvete de Creme com Calda de Goiabada (Cream Ice Cream with Guava Sauce)
- Xinxim de Galinha (Chicken and Shrimp Stew)
- Sarapatel (Pork Offal Stew)
- Rosquinhas de Coco (Coconut Cookies)
- Ambrosia (Brazilian Custard)
- Caruru (Okra Stew)
- Salada de Palmito (Hearts of Palm Salad)
- Sururu com Leite de Coco (Clams in Coconut Milk)
- Cocada Preta (Black Coconut Candy)
- Pamonha (Sweet Corn Tamale)
- Creme de Papaya com Cassis (Papaya Cream with Cassis Liqueur)
- Mingau de Milho Verde (Brazilian Green Corn Porridge)

Feijoada (Brazilian Black Bean Stew)

Ingredients:

- 500g dried black beans
- 500g assorted pork or beef cuts (such as pork shoulder, bacon, sausage, ribs, etc.)
- 1 onion, chopped
- 4 cloves garlic, minced
- 2 bay leaves
- Salt and pepper to taste
- 2 tablespoons vegetable oil
- Water
- Rice, for serving
- Farofa (toasted cassava flour), orange slices, and chopped parsley for garnish

Instructions:

Rinse the black beans thoroughly under cold water. Soak the beans overnight in a large bowl of water. Drain and rinse the beans before cooking.
In a large pot, heat the vegetable oil over medium heat. Add the chopped onion and minced garlic, and sauté until translucent.
Add the assorted pork or beef cuts to the pot and brown them on all sides.
Stir in the soaked black beans, bay leaves, and enough water to cover everything by about an inch.
Bring the mixture to a boil, then reduce the heat to low and simmer, partially covered, for about 2-3 hours or until the beans are tender and the meat is cooked through.
Periodically skim off any foam or impurities that rise to the surface of the stew.
Once the beans are cooked and the meat is tender, remove the bay leaves and season the feijoada with salt and pepper to taste.
Serve the feijoada hot with white rice, farofa, orange slices, and chopped parsley on the side. Enjoy!

Feijoada is often served with accompaniments such as orange slices, farofa (toasted cassava flour), and chopped parsley to balance its richness. Enjoy this comforting and flavorful Brazilian dish!

Pão de Queijo (Cheese Bread)

Ingredients:

- 2 cups tapioca flour (also known as tapioca starch)
- 1 cup milk
- 1/2 cup vegetable oil
- 1 teaspoon salt
- 2 cups grated cheese (traditionally, Queijo Minas or Parmesan cheese is used)
- 2 eggs

Instructions:

Preheat your oven to 375°F (190°C). Grease a mini muffin tin or line it with parchment paper.
In a saucepan, combine the milk, vegetable oil, and salt. Heat over medium heat until it just starts to boil.
Remove the saucepan from the heat and add the tapioca flour to the hot milk mixture. Stir well until the mixture comes together into a smooth dough.
Allow the dough to cool slightly, then add the grated cheese and eggs. Mix until everything is well combined and the cheese is evenly distributed throughout the dough.
Using a spoon or a cookie scoop, portion the dough into the prepared mini muffin tin, filling each cavity about three-quarters full.
Bake the pão de queijo in the preheated oven for 15-20 minutes, or until they are puffed up and golden brown on top.
Remove the pão de queijo from the oven and let them cool slightly before serving.
Serve the pão de queijo warm as a snack or as a side dish. Enjoy the cheesy goodness!

Pão de queijo is best enjoyed fresh out of the oven when they are warm and gooey. They are perfect for breakfast, brunch, or as a snack any time of the day.

Coxinha (Chicken Croquettes)

Ingredients:

For the dough:

- 2 cups chicken broth
- 2 cups all-purpose flour
- 2 tablespoons butter
- Salt to taste

For the chicken filling:

- 2 chicken breasts, cooked and shredded
- 1 onion, finely chopped
- 2 cloves garlic, minced
- 2 tablespoons olive oil
- 1 tablespoon tomato paste
- 1/2 cup chicken broth
- Salt and pepper to taste
- Chopped parsley or green onions for garnish (optional)

For breading and frying:

- 2 eggs, beaten
- Breadcrumbs
- Oil for frying

Instructions:

In a saucepan, bring the chicken broth and butter to a boil. Add salt to taste. Reduce the heat to low and gradually add the flour, stirring constantly, until a smooth dough forms. Cook for a few more minutes until the dough pulls away from the sides of the pan.
Remove the dough from the heat and let it cool slightly.
In a separate pan, heat the olive oil over medium heat. Sauté the chopped onion and garlic until translucent.

Add the shredded chicken to the pan and cook for a few minutes.
Stir in the tomato paste and chicken broth. Season with salt and pepper to taste.
Cook until the mixture is thickened and the flavors are well combined.
Remove the chicken filling from the heat and let it cool completely.
Take a small portion of the dough and flatten it in the palm of your hand. Place a spoonful of the chicken filling in the center and shape the dough around the filling into a teardrop shape, making sure to seal the edges well.
Dip the coxinha into the beaten eggs, then roll it in breadcrumbs until fully coated.
Heat the oil in a deep fryer or a heavy-bottomed pot to 350°F (175°C). Fry the coxinhas in batches until they are golden brown and crispy, about 5-7 minutes.
Remove the coxinhas from the oil and drain them on paper towels.
Serve the coxinhas hot, garnished with chopped parsley or green onions if desired. Enjoy your delicious Brazilian chicken croquettes!

Coxinhas are typically served as appetizers or snacks at parties, but they can also be enjoyed as a light meal. They are best when served hot and crispy.

Moqueca de Peixe (Brazilian Fish Stew)

Ingredients:

- 1.5 lbs (about 700g) firm white fish fillets (such as cod, tilapia, or halibut), cut into chunks
- 1 onion, thinly sliced
- 3 cloves garlic, minced
- 1 bell pepper, thinly sliced (any color you prefer)
- 2 tomatoes, diced
- 1 tablespoon tomato paste
- 1 can (14 oz or 400ml) coconut milk
- Juice of 1 lime
- 2 tablespoons olive oil
- 1/4 cup chopped cilantro or parsley
- Salt and pepper to taste
- Optional: sliced chili pepper for extra heat
- Cooked rice, for serving

Instructions:

In a large bowl, season the fish chunks with salt, pepper, and lime juice. Let them marinate for about 15-20 minutes while you prepare the other ingredients.
In a large skillet or Dutch oven, heat the olive oil over medium heat. Add the sliced onion and sauté until softened and translucent, about 3-4 minutes.
Add the minced garlic and sliced bell pepper to the skillet. Cook for another 2-3 minutes until fragrant.
Stir in the diced tomatoes and tomato paste. Cook for a few more minutes until the tomatoes start to break down and release their juices.
Pour in the coconut milk and stir well to combine all the ingredients. Bring the mixture to a gentle simmer.
Carefully add the marinated fish chunks to the skillet, making sure they are submerged in the coconut milk mixture. If desired, add sliced chili pepper for extra heat.
Cover the skillet and let the fish simmer in the coconut milk mixture for about 10-15 minutes, or until the fish is cooked through and flakes easily with a fork.
Taste the stew and adjust the seasoning with salt, pepper, and lime juice if needed.

Sprinkle chopped cilantro or parsley over the Moqueca de Peixe before serving. Serve the Moqueca de Peixe hot with cooked rice on the side. Enjoy this delicious Brazilian fish stew!

Moqueca de Peixe is a comforting and satisfying dish that is perfect for a cozy meal with family and friends. The combination of tender fish, creamy coconut milk, and aromatic spices makes it truly irresistible.

Brigadeiro (Chocolate Truffles)

Ingredients:

- 1 can (14 oz or 395g) sweetened condensed milk
- 3 tablespoons unsweetened cocoa powder
- 2 tablespoons unsalted butter
- Chocolate sprinkles, for coating

Instructions:

In a non-stick saucepan, combine the sweetened condensed milk, cocoa powder, and butter.
Cook the mixture over medium heat, stirring constantly with a wooden spoon or spatula to prevent burning and sticking.
Continue cooking and stirring until the mixture thickens and starts to pull away from the sides of the pan, forming a thick paste. This should take about 10-15 minutes.
Once the brigadeiro mixture is thickened and glossy, remove it from the heat and transfer it to a bowl. Let it cool to room temperature.
Once the brigadeiro mixture has cooled, lightly grease your hands with butter or oil to prevent sticking. Take small portions of the mixture and roll them into small balls between your palms to form the truffles.
Roll the brigadeiro balls in chocolate sprinkles until they are evenly coated.
Place the brigadeiro truffles on a parchment-lined baking sheet or a plate.
Repeat the process with the remaining brigadeiro mixture until you have rolled all of it into truffles.
Once all the truffles are formed and coated, refrigerate them for at least 30 minutes to firm up.
Serve the brigadeiro truffles chilled and enjoy their rich, chocolatey goodness!

Brigadeiro truffles are perfect for parties, celebrations, or as a sweet treat any time of the year. They can be stored in an airtight container in the refrigerator for several days. Simply bring them to room temperature before serving. Enjoy!

Churrasco (Brazilian BBQ)

Ingredients:

- Assorted meats (common choices include beef cuts like picanha, flank steak, sirloin, ribs, sausage, chicken, and pork)
- Coarse salt (rock salt) for seasoning
- Optional: marinades or seasoning blends for flavoring the meats
- Chimichurri sauce or other condiments for serving

Instructions:

Prepare the grill: If using a charcoal grill, light the charcoal and let it burn until the coals are hot and covered with ash. If using a gas grill, preheat it to medium-high heat. Make sure the grill grates are clean and lightly oiled to prevent sticking.

Season the meats: Season the meats generously with coarse salt. For added flavor, you can also marinate the meats in your favorite marinade or seasoning blend for a few hours or overnight before grilling.

Skewer the meats: Thread the seasoned meats onto skewers, alternating different cuts and types of meat if desired. Make sure not to overcrowd the skewers to ensure even cooking.

Grill the meats: Place the skewers on the preheated grill, positioning them directly over the flame or heat source. Cook the meats, turning occasionally, until they are cooked to your desired doneness. Brazilian churrasco is often served with meats cooked to varying levels of doneness, from rare to well-done, to accommodate different preferences.

Serve: Once the meats are cooked, transfer them to a serving platter or board. Serve the churrasco hot off the grill, accompanied by chimichurri sauce or other condiments for dipping or drizzling.

Enjoy: Gather your friends and family around the table and enjoy the flavorful meats of the Brazilian churrasco tradition. Don't forget to pair the barbecue with side dishes like rice, beans, farofa (toasted cassava flour), and salads to complete the meal.

Hosting a Brazilian churrasco is not just about the food—it's about the experience of coming together, sharing good food, and enjoying each other's company. So fire up the grill and get ready to indulge in the deliciousness of Brazilian barbecue!

Farofa (Toasted Cassava Flour)

Ingredients:

- 1 cup cassava flour (farinha de mandioca)
- 2-3 tablespoons butter or oil
- 1 onion, finely chopped
- 2 cloves garlic, minced
- Salt and pepper to taste
- Optional add-ins: chopped bacon, diced sausage, sliced olives, boiled eggs, chopped parsley or cilantro, diced banana or plantain

Instructions:

Heat a skillet or frying pan over medium heat. Add the butter or oil and let it melt or heat up.

Add the finely chopped onion to the skillet and sauté until it becomes translucent and starts to brown, about 3-5 minutes.

Add the minced garlic to the skillet and sauté for another 1-2 minutes until fragrant.

If using any optional add-ins like bacon or sausage, add them to the skillet and cook until they are browned and crispy.

Add the cassava flour (farinha de mandioca) to the skillet and stir well to combine with the other ingredients. Cook, stirring constantly, for about 5-7 minutes or until the cassava flour is lightly toasted and golden brown. Be careful not to burn it.

Season the farofa with salt and pepper to taste. If desired, you can also add any other optional seasonings or herbs at this point.

Remove the skillet from the heat and transfer the farofa to a serving dish.

Serve the farofa hot or at room temperature as a side dish alongside Brazilian meals. It pairs well with dishes like feijoada, churrasco, or grilled fish.

Farofa can be customized with various ingredients and flavors according to personal preference. It adds a delicious crunch and richness to meals and is a staple in Brazilian cuisine. Enjoy experimenting with different variations of farofa to find your favorite combination!

Caipirinha (Brazilian Cocktail)

Ingredients:

- 2 oz (60 ml) cachaça
- 1 lime, cut into wedges
- 2 teaspoons granulated sugar
- Ice cubes
- Lime slices or wedges for garnish (optional)

Instructions:

Start by placing the lime wedges and sugar in the bottom of a sturdy glass or cocktail shaker.

Use a muddler or the back of a spoon to muddle (or gently crush) the lime wedges and sugar together. This will release the lime juice and help dissolve the sugar.

Add the cachaça to the glass or cocktail shaker.

Fill the glass with ice cubes.

Stir or shake the mixture vigorously to combine all the ingredients and chill the drink.

Taste the Caipirinha and adjust the sweetness if necessary by adding more sugar if desired.

Garnish the Caipirinha with a slice or wedge of lime if desired.

Serve the Caipirinha immediately, either straight up or on the rocks, and enjoy its refreshing and tangy flavor!

Note: Traditional Caipirinhas are made with cachaça, which is a Brazilian spirit made from sugarcane juice. If you can't find cachaça, you can substitute it with rum, although it will alter the flavor slightly.

Caipirinhas are best enjoyed fresh and cold. They're a delightful cocktail to sip on during summer gatherings or to enjoy as a happy hour drink. Cheers!

Bobó de Camarão (Shrimp in Cassava Cream)

Ingredients:

- 1 lb (450g) large shrimp, peeled and deveined
- 2 cups cassava (yuca) or manioc, peeled and diced
- 1 can (13.5 oz or 400ml) coconut milk
- 1 onion, finely chopped
- 3 cloves garlic, minced
- 2 tomatoes, diced
- 1 bell pepper, diced
- 2 tablespoons olive oil
- 2 tablespoons chopped cilantro or parsley
- 1 tablespoon palm oil (optional, for color and flavor)
- 1 tablespoon lime juice
- Salt and pepper to taste
- Optional: sliced chili pepper for heat

Instructions:

Boil the diced cassava in salted water until tender, about 15-20 minutes. Drain and set aside.

In a blender or food processor, purée the boiled cassava with half of the coconut milk until smooth. Set aside.

In a large skillet or pot, heat the olive oil over medium heat. Add the chopped onion and sauté until translucent.

Add the minced garlic to the skillet and cook for another minute until fragrant.

Stir in the diced tomatoes and bell pepper. Cook until the vegetables are softened, about 5-7 minutes.

Add the puréed cassava mixture to the skillet, along with the remaining coconut milk and palm oil (if using). Stir well to combine.

Season the mixture with salt and pepper to taste. If using chili pepper, add it at this point for heat.

Bring the mixture to a simmer and let it cook for a few minutes to thicken slightly.

Add the peeled and deveined shrimp to the skillet and cook until they turn pink and are cooked through, about 5-7 minutes.

Stir in the lime juice and chopped cilantro or parsley.

Taste and adjust the seasoning if needed.

Serve the Bobó de Camarão hot, garnished with additional chopped cilantro or parsley if desired. Enjoy with rice or bread to soak up the creamy sauce!

Bobó de Camarão is a flavorful and comforting dish that highlights the tropical flavors of Brazil. It's perfect for special occasions or for a cozy dinner at home.

Acarajé (Black-Eyed Pea Fritters)

Ingredients:

For the Acarajé Fritters:

- 2 cups dried black-eyed peas
- Water for soaking
- 1 small onion, finely chopped
- 2 cloves garlic, minced
- 1 teaspoon salt
- Vegetable oil for frying

For the Vatapá Filling (optional):

- 1 cup dried shrimp, soaked in water for 30 minutes and drained
- 1 cup unsweetened coconut milk
- 2 slices of white bread, soaked in water and squeezed dry
- 1 small onion, chopped
- 2 cloves garlic, minced
- 1 tablespoon palm oil (dendê oil), plus extra for frying
- 1 teaspoon ground ginger
- 1 teaspoon ground coriander
- 1 teaspoon ground dried shrimp (optional)
- Salt to taste

For Serving:

- Hot pepper sauce (such as pimenta malagueta)
- Sliced green onions or cilantro for garnish

Instructions:

Place the dried black-eyed peas in a large bowl and cover them with water. Let them soak overnight or for at least 6 hours.

Drain the soaked black-eyed peas and transfer them to a food processor. Add the chopped onion, minced garlic, and salt. Process until you get a smooth, thick paste, adding a little water if necessary to help blend.

Heat vegetable oil in a deep fryer or a heavy-bottomed pot to 350°F (175°C).

Wet your hands with water and shape the black-eyed pea paste into small balls, about 2 inches in diameter.

Carefully drop the balls into the hot oil and fry them until they are golden brown and crispy on the outside, about 5-7 minutes. Make sure not to overcrowd the pot; fry in batches if necessary.

Remove the Acarajé fritters from the oil and drain them on paper towels.

If making the Vatapá filling, combine the soaked dried shrimp, coconut milk, soaked bread, chopped onion, minced garlic, palm oil, ground ginger, ground coriander, ground dried shrimp (if using), and salt in a blender or food processor. Blend until smooth.

Heat a little palm oil in a skillet over medium heat. Add the blended mixture to the skillet and cook, stirring constantly, until it thickens and becomes fragrant, about 10-15 minutes. Adjust seasoning with salt if needed.

To serve, split open the Acarajé fritters and fill them with a spoonful of the Vatapá filling. Optionally, drizzle with hot pepper sauce and garnish with sliced green onions or cilantro.

Serve the Acarajé hot and enjoy this delicious and iconic Brazilian street food!

Acarajé is a flavorful and satisfying snack that perfectly blends savory, spicy, and creamy flavors. It's a must-try for anyone looking to experience the diverse and vibrant cuisine of Brazil, especially the cuisine of Bahia.

Vatapá (Spicy Shrimp and Fish Stew)

Ingredients:

- 1 lb (450g) shrimp, peeled and deveined
- 1 lb (450g) firm white fish fillets (such as tilapia or cod), cut into chunks
- 1 cup unsweetened coconut milk
- 2 slices of white bread, crust removed
- 1 onion, chopped
- 2 cloves garlic, minced
- 1 red bell pepper, chopped
- 1 green bell pepper, chopped
- 1 tomato, chopped
- 2 tablespoons palm oil (dendê oil), plus extra for frying
- 1 tablespoon ground dried shrimp (optional)
- 1 tablespoon ground ginger
- 1 tablespoon ground coriander
- 1 tablespoon ground peanuts or cashews
- 1 tablespoon ground toasted coconut (optional)
- 1 teaspoon ground chili pepper (adjust to taste)
- Salt to taste
- Chopped cilantro or parsley for garnish

Instructions:

In a large skillet or pot, heat a tablespoon of palm oil over medium heat. Add the chopped onion, minced garlic, and bell peppers. Sauté until the vegetables are softened, about 5-7 minutes.

Add the chopped tomato to the skillet and cook for another 2-3 minutes until it starts to break down.

Tear the slices of bread into small pieces and soak them in water for a few minutes. Squeeze out excess water and set aside.

In a blender or food processor, combine the soaked bread, coconut milk, ground dried shrimp (if using), ground ginger, ground coriander, ground peanuts or cashews, ground toasted coconut (if using), ground chili pepper, and a pinch of salt. Blend until smooth.

Add the blended mixture to the skillet with the sautéed vegetables. Stir well to combine.

Add the shrimp and fish to the skillet, stirring gently to coat them with the sauce. Cook the mixture over medium-low heat, stirring occasionally, until the shrimp and fish are cooked through and the sauce has thickened, about 10-15 minutes.
Once the Vatapá is cooked, taste and adjust the seasoning with salt if needed.
In a separate skillet, heat a tablespoon of palm oil over medium heat. Add the shrimp and cook until they are pink and cooked through, about 2-3 minutes per side. Remove the shrimp from the skillet and set aside.
To serve, ladle the Vatapá into bowls and top each serving with a few cooked shrimp. Garnish with chopped cilantro or parsley.
Serve the Vatapá hot with steamed rice or traditional Brazilian side dishes like farofa or acarajé.

Enjoy the rich and spicy flavors of this traditional Brazilian dish!

Quindim (Coconut Custard)

Ingredients:

- 1 cup sweetened shredded coconut
- 1 cup granulated sugar
- 4 large egg yolks
- 1 tablespoon unsalted butter, melted
- 1/2 cup coconut milk
- 1/2 teaspoon vanilla extract
- Additional butter or oil for greasing the molds

Instructions:

Preheat your oven to 350°F (175°C). Grease 12 small ramekins or muffin tin cups with butter or oil.

In a bowl, combine the sweetened shredded coconut and granulated sugar. Mix well.

In a separate bowl, whisk together the egg yolks, melted butter, coconut milk, and vanilla extract until smooth.

Gradually add the egg yolk mixture to the coconut-sugar mixture, stirring until well combined.

Divide the mixture evenly among the greased ramekins or muffin tin cups, filling each about three-quarters full.

Place the ramekins or muffin tin on a baking sheet to catch any potential drips during baking.

Bake the quindim in the preheated oven for 25-30 minutes, or until set and the tops are golden brown.

Remove the quindim from the oven and let them cool in the ramekins or muffin tin for about 10 minutes.

Carefully run a knife around the edges of each quindim to loosen them from the molds. Then, invert the ramekins or muffin tin onto a serving platter to release the quindim.

Allow the quindim to cool completely before serving. They can be served at room temperature or chilled in the refrigerator.

Serve the quindim as a delightful dessert, either on its own or garnished with fresh fruit or whipped cream if desired.

Quindim is a wonderfully sweet and coconutty treat that is sure to impress your family and friends. Enjoy the tropical flavors of Brazil with this delicious dessert!

Arroz de Carreteiro (Brazilian Beef and Rice)

Ingredients:

- 1 lb (450g) beef chuck or other beef cut, diced into small pieces
- 2 cups white rice
- 4 cups beef broth or water
- 1 onion, chopped
- 3 cloves garlic, minced
- 1 bell pepper, chopped
- 2 tomatoes, diced
- 2 tablespoons vegetable oil
- 1 bay leaf
- Salt and pepper to taste
- Chopped parsley or green onions for garnish

Instructions:

In a large skillet or pot, heat the vegetable oil over medium heat. Add the diced beef and cook until browned on all sides.

Add the chopped onion and minced garlic to the skillet. Sauté until the onion becomes translucent.

Stir in the chopped bell pepper and diced tomatoes. Cook for a few minutes until the vegetables start to soften.

Add the white rice to the skillet and cook, stirring frequently, for a couple of minutes to toast the rice slightly.

Pour in the beef broth or water, and add the bay leaf. Season with salt and pepper to taste.

Bring the mixture to a boil, then reduce the heat to low. Cover the skillet or pot and simmer for about 15-20 minutes, or until the rice is cooked and the liquid is absorbed.

Once the rice is cooked, remove the bay leaf and stir the Arroz de Carreteiro to fluff it up.

Taste and adjust the seasoning if necessary.

Garnish the Arroz de Carreteiro with chopped parsley or green onions before serving.

Serve the Arroz de Carreteiro hot as a main dish, accompanied by a simple salad or cooked vegetables if desired.

Arroz de Carreteiro is a comforting and satisfying meal that is perfect for sharing with family and friends. Enjoy the rich flavors of Brazilian cuisine with this classic dish!

Pastel (Brazilian Pastries)

Ingredients:

For the dough:

- 2 cups all-purpose flour
- 1/2 teaspoon salt
- 2 tablespoons vegetable oil
- 3/4 cup warm water

For the filling:

- Your choice of savory fillings, such as ground beef, shredded chicken, cheese, ham, or vegetables
- Seasonings and spices to taste (e.g., salt, pepper, garlic powder, onion powder)

For frying:

- Vegetable oil for deep-frying

Instructions:

In a large bowl, whisk together the flour and salt. Gradually add the vegetable oil and warm water, stirring until a dough forms.

Knead the dough on a floured surface for a few minutes until it becomes smooth and elastic. Cover the dough with a damp cloth and let it rest for about 30 minutes.

While the dough is resting, prepare your choice of filling. Cook any raw fillings (such as ground beef or vegetables) with seasonings and spices until fully cooked and flavorful. Let the filling cool completely before using.

After the dough has rested, divide it into small portions (about the size of a golf ball) and roll each portion into a thin circle or rectangle, about 1/8 inch thick.

Place a spoonful of the prepared filling onto one half of each dough circle or rectangle, leaving a small border around the edges.

Fold the other half of the dough over the filling to enclose it, then use a fork to crimp the edges firmly to seal.

Heat vegetable oil in a deep fryer or large skillet to 350°F (175°C).
Carefully place the filled pastries into the hot oil, a few at a time, and fry until golden brown and crispy, about 2-3 minutes per side.
Remove the fried pastries from the oil using a slotted spoon and drain them on paper towels to remove excess oil.
Serve the pastel hot and crispy, either as is or with your favorite dipping sauce or condiments.

Pastel is a versatile and delicious snack that can be enjoyed any time of day. You can customize the fillings to suit your preferences, making them perfect for parties, gatherings, or as a quick and satisfying meal on the go. Enjoy!

Beijinho (Coconut Truffles)

Ingredients:

- 1 can (14 oz or 395g) sweetened condensed milk
- 1 tablespoon unsalted butter
- 1 cup sweetened shredded coconut, plus extra for coating
- Cloves or chocolate sprinkles for decoration (optional)

Instructions:

In a non-stick saucepan, combine the sweetened condensed milk, butter, and shredded coconut.
Cook the mixture over medium heat, stirring constantly, until it thickens and starts to pull away from the sides of the pan. This should take about 10-15 minutes.
Remove the mixture from the heat and let it cool to room temperature.
Once the mixture has cooled, grease your hands with butter or oil to prevent sticking. Take small portions of the mixture and roll them into balls between your palms.
Roll each ball in sweetened shredded coconut to coat it evenly.
If desired, insert a clove into the top of each beijinho for decoration, or roll them in chocolate sprinkles.
Place the beijinhos on a tray lined with parchment paper and refrigerate them for at least 30 minutes to firm up.
Once firm, transfer the beijinhos to an airtight container and store them in the refrigerator until ready to serve.
Serve the beijinhos chilled and enjoy their sweet and coconutty flavor!

Beijinhos are perfect for parties, celebrations, or as a sweet treat any time of the day.

They are simple to make and sure to be a hit with everyone who tries them!

Escondidinho de Carne Seca (Cassava and Jerky Casserole)

Ingredients:

For the mashed cassava:

- 2 lbs (about 1 kg) cassava (yuca or manioc), peeled and cut into chunks
- Water
- Salt to taste
- 2 tablespoons butter
- 1/2 cup milk (optional)

For the carne seca filling:

- 1 lb (about 450g) dried beef (carne seca)
- 1 onion, chopped
- 3 cloves garlic, minced
- 2 tomatoes, diced
- 1 bell pepper, diced
- 2 tablespoons vegetable oil
- Salt and pepper to taste
- Chopped cilantro or parsley for garnish (optional)

For assembling:

- 1 cup shredded cheese (such as mozzarella or cheddar)

Instructions:

Prepare the dried beef (carne seca) by soaking it in water overnight to remove excess salt. Drain and shred the beef.

In a large pot, boil the cassava chunks in salted water until tender, about 20-25 minutes. Drain the cassava and transfer it to a large bowl.

Mash the cooked cassava with a potato masher or fork until smooth. Add the butter and milk (if using) to the mashed cassava and mix well. Season with salt to taste. Set aside.

In a skillet, heat the vegetable oil over medium heat. Add the chopped onion and minced garlic, and sauté until translucent.

Add the shredded dried beef to the skillet and cook for a few minutes until heated through.

Stir in the diced tomatoes and bell pepper, and cook for another 5-7 minutes until the vegetables are softened. Season with salt and pepper to taste. Remove from heat.

Preheat your oven to 375°F (190°C). Grease a baking dish with butter or oil.

Spread half of the mashed cassava mixture evenly into the bottom of the prepared baking dish.

Layer the cooked carne seca filling on top of the mashed cassava layer.

Sprinkle half of the shredded cheese over the carne seca layer.

Spread the remaining mashed cassava mixture over the carne seca layer, smoothing it out with a spatula.

Sprinkle the remaining shredded cheese over the top of the casserole.

Bake the Escondidinho de Carne Seca in the preheated oven for 25-30 minutes, or until the cheese is melted and bubbly and the casserole is heated through.

Remove the casserole from the oven and let it cool slightly before serving.

Garnish the Escondidinho de Carne Seca with chopped cilantro or parsley, if desired.

Serve the casserole hot and enjoy this comforting Brazilian dish!

Escondidinho de Carne Seca is a delicious and satisfying meal that's sure to be a hit with your family and friends. Enjoy the layers of creamy mashed cassava, flavorful carne seca, and melted cheese in every bite!

Cocada (Coconut Candy)

Ingredients:

- 2 cups shredded coconut (fresh or dried)
- 1 cup granulated sugar
- 1/2 cup water
- 1/2 teaspoon vanilla extract (optional)
- Pinch of salt
- Ground cinnamon or cloves for flavoring (optional)

Instructions:

In a medium saucepan, combine the sugar, water, vanilla extract (if using), and pinch of salt. Stir well to dissolve the sugar.

Place the saucepan over medium heat and bring the mixture to a boil, stirring occasionally.

Once the mixture comes to a boil, reduce the heat to low and add the shredded coconut to the saucepan. Stir well to combine.

Continue cooking the mixture over low heat, stirring frequently, until it thickens and the coconut absorbs the syrup, about 10-15 minutes. The cocada should have a sticky and slightly thick consistency.

If using, add ground cinnamon or cloves to the cocada for additional flavor, stirring to incorporate.

Once the cocada reaches the desired consistency and flavor, remove the saucepan from the heat.

Line a baking sheet or tray with parchment paper or greased foil.

Using a spoon or small ice cream scoop, drop small portions of the cocada mixture onto the prepared baking sheet, leaving some space between each portion.

Allow the cocada to cool and firm up at room temperature for at least 30 minutes.

Once cooled and set, the cocada can be enjoyed immediately or stored in an airtight container at room temperature for several days.

Serve the cocada as a sweet treat on its own, or use it as a topping for desserts like ice cream or cakes.

Cocada is a simple yet delightful candy that showcases the tropical flavors of coconut. Whether enjoyed as a snack or dessert, it's sure to satisfy your sweet tooth with its irresistible sweetness and chewy texture.

Caldo Verde (Brazilian Green Soup)

Ingredients:

- 4 medium potatoes, peeled and diced
- 1 onion, finely chopped
- 2 cloves garlic, minced
- 4 cups chicken or vegetable broth
- 1 bunch kale, stems removed and leaves thinly sliced
- 1/2 lb (225g) chorizo sausage, thinly sliced (optional)
- 2 tablespoons olive oil
- Salt and pepper to taste

Instructions:

In a large pot, heat the olive oil over medium heat. Add the chopped onion and minced garlic, and sauté until softened and fragrant, about 3-4 minutes.
Add the diced potatoes to the pot and sauté for another 2-3 minutes, stirring occasionally.
Pour the chicken or vegetable broth into the pot, covering the potatoes and onions. Bring the mixture to a boil, then reduce the heat to low and let it simmer until the potatoes are tender, about 15-20 minutes.
Once the potatoes are cooked, use an immersion blender or potato masher to partially mash the potatoes in the pot, leaving some chunks for texture.
Add the thinly sliced kale to the pot and stir well to combine. Let the soup simmer for another 5-7 minutes, or until the kale is wilted and tender.
If using chorizo sausage, add it to the pot during the last few minutes of cooking to heat through.
Season the Caldo Verde with salt and pepper to taste, adjusting the seasoning as needed.
Ladle the hot Caldo Verde into bowls and serve immediately.

Caldo Verde is often enjoyed with crusty bread on the side for dipping or as a light meal on its own. It's a comforting and nutritious soup that's sure to warm you up on chilly days. Enjoy!

Canjica (Brazilian Sweet Corn Pudding)

Ingredients:

- 2 cups dried white corn kernels (canjica)
- Water for soaking
- 6 cups whole milk
- 1 cup sugar (adjust to taste)
- 1 cinnamon stick
- 4 cloves
- Pinch of salt
- Cinnamon powder for garnish (optional)

Instructions:

Rinse the dried white corn kernels (canjica) under cold water and then soak them in water overnight, or for at least 8 hours.

After soaking, drain the corn kernels and rinse them again under cold water.

In a large pot, combine the soaked corn kernels, whole milk, cinnamon stick, cloves, and a pinch of salt.

Bring the mixture to a boil over medium-high heat, then reduce the heat to low and let it simmer, partially covered, stirring occasionally, for about 1.5 to 2 hours, or until the corn kernels are tender and the mixture has thickened. Add more milk if needed to achieve the desired consistency.

Once the corn kernels are tender and the mixture has thickened, stir in the sugar and continue to cook for another 15-20 minutes, or until the sugar has dissolved and the mixture is sweetened to your liking.

Remove the pot from the heat and let the canjica cool slightly.

Serve the canjica warm or chilled in individual bowls, garnished with a sprinkle of cinnamon powder if desired.

Enjoy this comforting and sweet Brazilian dessert!

Note: Canjica can be stored in the refrigerator for a few days. If reheating, you may need to add a splash of milk to loosen the mixture as it tends to thicken when chilled.

Empadão (Brazilian Meat Pie)

Ingredients:

For the pastry crust:

- 3 cups all-purpose flour
- 1 cup unsalted butter, cold and cubed
- 1 teaspoon salt
- 1 egg
- 2-3 tablespoons ice water

For the filling:

- 1 lb (about 450g) ground beef or chicken
- 1 onion, chopped
- 2 cloves garlic, minced
- 1 bell pepper, diced
- 2 tomatoes, diced
- 1/2 cup frozen peas
- 1/2 cup sliced olives
- 1/2 cup shredded cheese (such as mozzarella or cheddar)
- 2 tablespoons vegetable oil
- Salt and pepper to taste
- Chopped parsley or green onions for garnish (optional)

Instructions:

Preheat your oven to 375°F (190°C). Grease a 9-inch pie dish or baking dish with butter or oil.

In a large mixing bowl, combine the all-purpose flour and salt. Add the cold cubed butter and use a pastry cutter or fork to cut the butter into the flour until the mixture resembles coarse crumbs.

In a small bowl, beat the egg with 2 tablespoons of ice water. Gradually add the egg mixture to the flour mixture, stirring with a fork until the dough comes together. If the dough is too dry, add additional ice water, one tablespoon at a time, until it forms a cohesive ball.

Divide the dough into two equal portions, one slightly larger than the other. Wrap each portion in plastic wrap and refrigerate for at least 30 minutes.

While the dough is chilling, prepare the filling. In a skillet, heat the vegetable oil over medium heat. Add the chopped onion and minced garlic, and sauté until softened and fragrant, about 3-4 minutes.

Add the ground beef or chicken to the skillet and cook until browned, breaking it up with a spoon as it cooks.

Stir in the diced bell pepper and tomatoes, and cook for another 5-7 minutes until the vegetables are softened.

Add the frozen peas and sliced olives to the skillet, and cook for a few more minutes until heated through. Season the filling with salt and pepper to taste. Remove from heat and let it cool slightly.

Roll out the larger portion of the chilled pastry dough on a lightly floured surface into a circle large enough to line the bottom and sides of the prepared pie dish.

Transfer the rolled-out dough to the pie dish, pressing it gently into the bottom and sides. Trim any excess dough hanging over the edges.

Spoon the cooled filling mixture into the pastry-lined pie dish, spreading it out evenly.

Sprinkle the shredded cheese over the filling.

Roll out the remaining chilled pastry dough into a circle large enough to cover the top of the pie dish.

Place the rolled-out dough over the filling, pressing the edges to seal with the bottom crust. Use a sharp knife to make a few slits in the top crust to allow steam to escape during baking.

Beat the remaining egg with a little water to make an egg wash. Brush the top crust with the egg wash.

Bake the Empadão in the preheated oven for 30-35 minutes, or until the crust is golden brown and the filling is bubbling.

Remove the pie from the oven and let it cool for a few minutes before slicing. Garnish the Empadão with chopped parsley or green onions, if desired.

Serve the Empadão warm as a delicious main dish, accompanied by a salad or your favorite side dishes.

Empadão is a comforting and flavorful dish that's perfect for sharing with family and friends. Enjoy the delicious combination of flaky pastry crust and savory meat filling in every bite!

Pé-de-Moleque (Peanut Brittle)

Ingredients:

- 2 cups raw peanuts (with or without skin)
- 1 cup granulated sugar
- Pinch of salt (optional)
- Butter or oil for greasing the pan

Instructions:

Grease a baking sheet or large tray with butter or oil and set aside.
In a heavy-bottomed skillet or saucepan, combine the raw peanuts and granulated sugar over medium heat.
Stir the mixture constantly with a wooden spoon or heat-resistant spatula as the sugar begins to melt and caramelize.
Continue cooking and stirring until the sugar melts completely and turns a deep golden brown color, and the peanuts are evenly coated with the caramelized sugar. This should take about 10-15 minutes.
If using salt, sprinkle a pinch over the mixture and stir to incorporate.
Once the peanuts are caramelized and evenly coated with sugar, immediately pour the mixture onto the greased baking sheet or tray.
Use the back of the spoon or spatula to spread the mixture out into an even layer, pressing down gently to compact it.
Let the Pé-de-Moleque cool completely at room temperature until it hardens and becomes crispy.
Once cooled and set, use a sharp knife to cut the Pé-de-Moleque into small squares or rectangles.
Serve the Pé-de-Moleque as a sweet snack or dessert, and enjoy its crunchy texture and rich peanut flavor!

Pé-de-Moleque is a classic Brazilian treat that's perfect for snacking on any time of day. It's simple to make and requires just a few ingredients, making it a popular choice for homemade sweets. Enjoy this delicious peanut brittle as a delightful indulgence!

Salpicão (Brazilian Chicken Salad)

Ingredients:

For the salad:

- 2 cups cooked chicken breast, shredded
- 1 cup carrots, grated
- 1 cup green apples, diced
- 1 cup canned pineapple, diced
- 1 cup canned sweet corn kernels
- 1 cup green peas (fresh or frozen), cooked
- 1/2 cup raisins
- 1/2 cup canned sliced or chopped olives
- 1/2 cup chopped fresh parsley or cilantro
- 1/2 cup chopped roasted peanuts or cashews (optional)
- Salt and pepper to taste

For the dressing:

- 1/2 cup mayonnaise
- 1/4 cup plain yogurt or sour cream
- 2 tablespoons lime juice
- 1 tablespoon Dijon mustard
- 1 teaspoon honey or sugar
- Salt and pepper to taste

Instructions:

In a large mixing bowl, combine the shredded chicken, grated carrots, diced green apples, diced pineapple, sweet corn kernels, cooked green peas, raisins, chopped olives, chopped parsley or cilantro, and chopped roasted peanuts or cashews (if using). Mix well to combine.

In a separate small bowl, whisk together the mayonnaise, plain yogurt or sour cream, lime juice, Dijon mustard, honey or sugar, and salt and pepper to taste. Adjust the seasoning and consistency of the dressing according to your preference.

Pour the dressing over the salad ingredients in the large mixing bowl.
Gently toss the salad until all the ingredients are evenly coated with the dressing.
Taste the salad and adjust the seasoning if necessary with more salt, pepper, or lime juice.
Once the salad is well combined and seasoned to your liking, cover the bowl with plastic wrap and refrigerate for at least 1 hour to allow the flavors to meld together.
Before serving, give the salad a final toss and transfer it to a serving bowl or platter.
Garnish the Salpicão with additional chopped parsley or cilantro, and serve chilled.

Salpicão is a refreshing and flavorful salad that is perfect for serving at picnics, barbecues, or as a side dish for holiday meals. Enjoy its combination of crunchy vegetables, sweet fruits, and creamy dressing!

Baião de Dois (Rice and Black-Eyed Peas)

Ingredients:

- 1 cup black-eyed peas (feijão-de-corda), soaked overnight or for at least 6 hours
- 1 cup white rice
- 4 cups water or broth
- 1 onion, chopped
- 2 cloves garlic, minced
- 2 tablespoons vegetable oil or olive oil
- 200g smoked sausage (linguiça), sliced
- 200g bacon, diced
- 1 tomato, diced
- 1/2 cup chopped cilantro or parsley
- Salt and pepper to taste
- Optional: 1/2 cup coconut milk

Instructions:

In a large pot, bring the soaked black-eyed peas to a boil in enough water to cover them. Reduce the heat to low and simmer until the peas are tender, about 30-40 minutes. Drain and set aside.
In a separate pot, heat the vegetable oil over medium heat. Add the diced bacon and sliced sausage to the pot and cook until browned and crispy, about 5-7 minutes.
Add the chopped onion and minced garlic to the pot with the bacon and sausage. Sauté until the onion becomes translucent and fragrant, about 3-4 minutes.
Stir in the diced tomato and cook for another 2-3 minutes until softened.
Add the cooked black-eyed peas to the pot along with the white rice. Stir to combine.
Pour in the water or broth, ensuring that the liquid covers the rice and peas by about 1 inch.
Season the mixture with salt and pepper to taste. If using coconut milk, add it to the pot at this point.
Bring the mixture to a boil, then reduce the heat to low. Cover the pot and let the Baião de Dois simmer until the rice is cooked and the liquid is absorbed, about 20-25 minutes.
Once the rice is cooked, remove the pot from the heat and let it sit, covered, for a few minutes.

Fluff the Baião de Dois with a fork and stir in the chopped cilantro or parsley. Serve the Baião de Dois hot as a main dish or side dish, garnished with additional chopped cilantro or parsley if desired.

Baião de Dois is a delicious and satisfying dish that combines the flavors of beans, rice, and meats into a comforting one-pot meal. Enjoy this traditional Brazilian recipe with family and friends!

Maria-mole (Coconut Marshmallows)

Ingredients:

- 3 cups shredded unsweetened coconut
- 2 cups granulated sugar
- 1 cup water
- 4 packets (28g) unflavored gelatin
- 1/2 cup cold water
- 1 teaspoon vanilla extract
- Vegetable oil or butter for greasing

Instructions:

Grease a square baking dish or pan (about 8x8 inches) with vegetable oil or butter and set aside.
In a large mixing bowl, combine the shredded coconut and granulated sugar. Mix well and set aside.
In a small bowl, sprinkle the unflavored gelatin over 1/2 cup of cold water. Let it sit for a few minutes to bloom.
In a saucepan, bring 1 cup of water to a boil. Once boiling, remove from heat and stir in the bloomed gelatin until completely dissolved.
Pour the hot gelatin mixture into the bowl with the coconut and sugar mixture.
Add the vanilla extract and mix until everything is well combined and the sugar is dissolved.
Pour the mixture into the greased baking dish or pan, spreading it out evenly with a spatula or the back of a spoon.
Let the Maria-mole cool and set at room temperature for at least 2-3 hours, or until firm.
Once the Maria-mole is set, use a sharp knife to cut it into squares or rectangles.
Serve the Maria-mole as a sweet treat or dessert, and enjoy its soft and chewy coconut flavor!
Store any leftovers in an airtight container at room temperature for up to several days.

Maria-mole is a simple and delicious dessert that's perfect for satisfying your sweet tooth. Enjoy its tropical coconut flavor and soft texture with family and friends!

Angu (Brazilian Polenta)

Ingredients:

- 1 cup cornmeal (coarse or fine)
- 4 cups water or milk
- Salt to taste
- Butter or olive oil for serving (optional)

Instructions:

In a saucepan, bring the water or milk to a boil over medium-high heat.
Once the liquid is boiling, gradually whisk in the cornmeal, stirring constantly to prevent lumps from forming.
Reduce the heat to low and continue to cook the mixture, stirring frequently, until it thickens to the desired consistency. This can take anywhere from 10 to 20 minutes, depending on the type of cornmeal used.
Season the angu with salt to taste, adjusting the amount according to your preference.
Once the angu is thickened and cooked to your liking, remove it from the heat.
Serve the angu hot as a side dish, topped with butter or olive oil if desired.
Angu can also be allowed to cool and set in a dish before being sliced and fried or grilled until crispy. This variation is known as "angu frito" and makes a delicious appetizer or snack.
Enjoy the angu as a comforting and versatile dish!

Angu is a simple and hearty dish that pairs well with a variety of savory accompaniments, such as meat stews, braised vegetables, or sautéed greens. It's a staple in Brazilian cuisine and can be adapted to suit your taste preferences and dietary needs.

Bolinho de Bacalhau (Codfish Balls)

Ingredients:

- 500g salted codfish (bacalhau)
- 500g potatoes, peeled and diced
- 1 onion, finely chopped
- 2 cloves of garlic, minced
- 1 bunch of fresh parsley, finely chopped
- 2 eggs
- 1 cup of all-purpose flour
- Salt and pepper to taste
- Oil for frying

Instructions:

Prepare the Codfish:
- Start by soaking the salted codfish in cold water overnight or for at least 12 hours to remove excess salt. Change the water a few times during this process.
- After soaking, rinse the codfish under cold water and pat it dry with paper towels. Remove any bones and skin, then flake the codfish into small pieces.

Cook the Potatoes:
- Boil the diced potatoes in a large pot of salted water until they are tender. Drain the potatoes and mash them until smooth.

Mix the Ingredients:
- In a large mixing bowl, combine the mashed potatoes, flaked codfish, chopped onion, minced garlic, chopped parsley, eggs, and flour. Season with salt and pepper to taste. Mix everything until well combined.

Form the Balls:
- Take small portions of the mixture and roll them into small balls, about the size of a golf ball. You can wet your hands slightly to prevent sticking.

Fry the Bolinhos:
- Heat oil in a deep frying pan or pot over medium heat. Once the oil is hot, carefully place the codfish balls into the oil, in batches if necessary, making sure not to overcrowd the pan.
- Fry the bolinhos until they are golden brown and crispy on the outside, turning them occasionally to ensure even cooking. This usually takes about 3-4 minutes per batch.

- Once cooked, remove the bolinhos from the oil and place them on a plate lined with paper towels to drain any excess oil.

Serve:
- Bolinho de Bacalhau is best served hot and crispy. You can enjoy them on their own or with a dipping sauce of your choice, such as aioli, tartar sauce, or hot sauce.

Enjoy!
- Serve the codfish balls as a delicious appetizer or snack for your family and friends to enjoy.

This recipe can be adjusted according to your taste preferences, so feel free to add other ingredients such as spices or herbs to enhance the flavor. Enjoy your Bolinho de Bacalhau!

Manjar Branco (Coconut Pudding)

Ingredients:

For the Manjar:

- 1 liter (4 cups) of coconut milk
- 200g (1 cup) of sugar
- 100g (2/3 cup) of cornstarch
- 100g (2/3 cup) of shredded coconut (optional)
- 1 teaspoon of vanilla extract

For the Sauce (optional):

- 200g (1 cup) of sugar
- 200ml (3/4 cup) of water
- 200g (1 1/2 cups) of fresh or frozen fruit (such as berries, mango, or passion fruit pulp)

Instructions:

Making the Manjar:

In a saucepan, combine the coconut milk, sugar, and shredded coconut (if using). Stir well to dissolve the sugar.
In a small bowl, mix the cornstarch with a little water to make a smooth paste. Gradually pour the cornstarch mixture into the saucepan with the coconut milk, stirring constantly to prevent lumps from forming.
Place the saucepan over medium heat and continue stirring until the mixture thickens and comes to a gentle boil. This usually takes about 10-15 minutes.
Once the mixture has thickened, remove it from the heat and stir in the vanilla extract.
Lightly grease a mold or individual ramekins with a neutral-flavored oil.
Pour the manjar mixture into the prepared mold or ramekins. Smooth the top with a spatula.
Allow the manjar to cool to room temperature, then refrigerate it for at least 4 hours or until set.

Making the Sauce (optional):

In a saucepan, combine the sugar and water to make a simple syrup.

Bring the syrup to a boil over medium heat, stirring occasionally, until the sugar has completely dissolved.

Add the fresh or frozen fruit to the syrup and continue cooking until the fruit softens and the mixture thickens slightly, about 5-10 minutes.

Remove the sauce from the heat and allow it to cool slightly.

Serving:

To serve, unmold the manjar onto a serving platter or onto individual plates.

If using the fruit sauce, spoon it over the top of the manjar.

Alternatively, you can serve the manjar with caramel sauce, coconut flakes, or fresh fruit.

Slice and serve the Manjar Branco chilled.

Enjoy this delightful Brazilian dessert with its creamy coconut flavor and sweet sauce!

Bolo de Fubá (Cornmeal Cake)

Ingredients:

- 1 cup (200g) fine cornmeal (fubá)
- 1 cup (125g) all-purpose flour
- 1 cup (200g) granulated sugar
- 1/2 cup (120ml) vegetable oil
- 3 eggs
- 1 cup (240ml) milk
- 1 tablespoon baking powder
- Pinch of salt
- Zest of 1 lemon or orange (optional)
- Butter or oil, for greasing the pan

Instructions:

Preheat your oven to 180°C (350°F). Grease a round cake pan (about 22-24cm in diameter) with butter or oil and dust it lightly with flour, tapping out any excess.
In a large mixing bowl, whisk together the eggs and sugar until light and fluffy.
Gradually add the vegetable oil while continuing to whisk until well combined.
Mix in the milk and lemon or orange zest (if using) until incorporated.
In a separate bowl, sift together the fine cornmeal (fubá), all-purpose flour, baking powder, and salt.
Gradually add the dry ingredients to the wet ingredients, mixing until you have a smooth batter. Be careful not to overmix.
Pour the batter into the prepared cake pan and spread it evenly.
Bake in the preheated oven for about 30-35 minutes, or until a toothpick inserted into the center comes out clean and the top is golden brown.
Remove the cake from the oven and let it cool in the pan for about 10 minutes.
Once cooled slightly, transfer the cake to a wire rack to cool completely.
Slice and serve the Bolo de Fubá plain or dusted with powdered sugar, if desired. It's also delicious with a cup of coffee or tea.
Enjoy your homemade Bolo de Fubá!

This cake is best enjoyed fresh on the day it's made but can also be stored in an airtight container at room temperature for a few days.

Cuscuz Paulista (Savory Cornmeal Pudding)

Ingredients:

For the Pudding:

- 2 cups fine cornmeal (fubá)
- 2 cups chicken or vegetable broth
- 1 cup water
- 1/2 cup cooked peas
- 1/2 cup cooked corn kernels
- 1/2 cup diced carrots
- 1/2 cup diced bell peppers (red, green, or yellow)
- 1/2 cup diced ham or sausage (optional)
- 1/2 cup sliced olives (green or black)
- 1/4 cup chopped parsley or cilantro
- Salt and pepper to taste
- Oil or butter for greasing the mold

For Garnish:

- Hard-boiled eggs, sliced
- Tomato slices
- Lettuce leaves

Instructions:

Prepare the Ingredients:
- Cook the peas, corn kernels, diced carrots, and diced bell peppers until tender. Drain any excess water and set aside.
- If using ham or sausage, cook and dice it into small pieces. Set aside.

Prepare the Pudding Mixture:
- In a large bowl, mix the fine cornmeal (fubá) with the chicken or vegetable broth and water. Stir until well combined and smooth.

Add the Vegetables and Seasonings:
- Add the cooked peas, corn kernels, diced carrots, diced bell peppers, diced ham or sausage (if using), sliced olives, chopped parsley or cilantro, salt, and pepper to the cornmeal mixture. Stir until all the ingredients are evenly distributed.

Grease the Mold:
- Grease a mold or pudding basin with oil or butter to prevent sticking.

Assemble the Pudding:
- Pour the pudding mixture into the greased mold, pressing it down gently with the back of a spoon to compact it.

Steam the Pudding:
- Place the mold in a large pot with enough water to reach halfway up the sides of the mold.
- Cover the pot with a lid and steam the pudding over medium heat for about 30-40 minutes, or until the pudding is firm and set.

Cool and Unmold:
- Once cooked, remove the pudding from the pot and let it cool slightly.
- To unmold, run a knife around the edges of the pudding and invert it onto a serving plate.

Serve:
- Garnish the Cuscuz Paulista with slices of hard-boiled eggs, tomato slices, and lettuce leaves, if desired.
- Slice and serve the pudding warm or at room temperature.

Enjoy your Cuscuz Paulista!

This savory cornmeal pudding makes for a hearty and satisfying meal, perfect for lunch or dinner. It can be enjoyed on its own or accompanied by salad or other side dishes.

Mungunzá (Brazilian Corn and Coconut Pudding)

Ingredients:

- 1 cup dried corn kernels (canjica or hominy)
- 1 can (400ml) coconut milk
- 4 cups water
- 1 cup granulated sugar
- 1 cinnamon stick
- Pinch of salt
- Cinnamon powder for garnish (optional)

Instructions:

Prepare the Corn Kernels:
- Rinse the dried corn kernels thoroughly under cold water.
- Soak the corn kernels in water overnight or for at least 8 hours to soften.

Cook the Corn Kernels:
- After soaking, drain the corn kernels and transfer them to a large pot.
- Add 4 cups of water to the pot along with the drained corn kernels.
- Bring the water to a boil over medium-high heat, then reduce the heat to low and simmer gently for about 1 to 1.5 hours, or until the corn kernels are tender. Stir occasionally and add more water if necessary to prevent sticking.

Add the Coconut Milk and Sugar:
- Once the corn kernels are tender, add the coconut milk, granulated sugar, cinnamon stick, and a pinch of salt to the pot.
- Stir well to combine and continue cooking over low heat for another 20-30 minutes, stirring occasionally, until the mixture thickens slightly and the flavors meld together.

Serve:
- Once the Mungunzá is ready, remove the cinnamon stick and discard it.
- Serve the Mungunzá warm or chilled in individual bowls.
- Optionally, sprinkle some cinnamon powder on top of each serving for extra flavor and garnish.

Enjoy your Mungunzá!

This creamy and flavorful Brazilian dessert is perfect for enjoying on its own or as part of a festive celebration. It's comforting, sweet, and full of delicious coconut and corn flavors.

Carne de Sol (Sun-Dried Beef)

Ingredients:

- 2 pounds (about 1 kg) of beef sirloin or rump steak
- Coarse salt (rock salt or kosher salt)
- Black pepper (optional)
- Garlic powder (optional)

Instructions:

Prepare the Beef:
- Start by trimming any excess fat from the beef sirloin or rump steak. You want to use lean meat for Carne de Sol.
- Cut the beef into thick slices or chunks, about 1 to 2 inches thick.

Salt the Beef:
- Generously coat each piece of beef with coarse salt on all sides. Make sure to rub the salt into the meat to ensure even seasoning.
- Optionally, you can add black pepper and garlic powder to the salt for additional flavor.

Cure the Beef:
- Place the salted beef pieces on a large tray or baking sheet lined with parchment paper or plastic wrap. Make sure the beef pieces are spread out and not touching each other.
- Leave the beef to cure in a cool, dry, and well-ventilated area for about 1 to 2 days. This can be done indoors or outdoors if you have a sunny and dry location.
- During this time, the beef will release moisture and become firmer as it cures. Turn the beef pieces occasionally to ensure even drying.

Finish Drying the Beef:
- After 1 to 2 days, the beef should have a firm texture and a darker color, indicating that it's ready.
- If desired, you can further dry the beef in a low-temperature oven (around 200°F or 95°C) for a few hours to remove any remaining moisture. This step is optional but can help prolong the shelf life of the Carne de Sol.

Store or Use the Carne de Sol:
- Once dried, the Carne de Sol can be stored in an airtight container or wrapped tightly in plastic wrap and refrigerated for up to a week.

- To use Carne de Sol in recipes, it's typically rehydrated by soaking it in water for a few hours or overnight before cooking. This helps to soften the meat and remove excess salt.

Cook and Enjoy:
- Carne de Sol can be used in various recipes, such as stews, fried dishes, or grilled skewers. It adds a unique flavor and texture to Brazilian cuisine.

Enjoy your homemade Carne de Sol!

Note: The curing process is crucial for Carne de Sol, as it helps to preserve the meat and develop its characteristic flavor. Be sure to use enough salt and allow enough time for the beef to cure properly. Adjust curing time based on factors such as humidity and temperature.

Sopa Leão Veloso (Brazilian Chicken Soup)

Ingredients:

- 1 whole chicken (about 3-4 pounds), cut into pieces
- 2 liters (about 8 cups) water
- 2 onions, chopped
- 3 cloves garlic, minced
- 2 carrots, diced
- 2 potatoes, diced
- 2 stalks celery, chopped
- 1 cup green peas (fresh or frozen)
- 1 cup corn kernels (fresh or frozen)
- 1 bay leaf
- Salt and pepper to taste
- Fresh parsley or cilantro, chopped, for garnish
- Cooked rice or noodles (optional, for serving)

Instructions:

Prepare the Chicken:
- Rinse the chicken pieces under cold water and pat them dry with paper towels.
- In a large pot, place the chicken pieces and cover them with water. Bring to a boil over high heat, then reduce the heat to low and simmer for about 30 minutes, skimming any foam that rises to the surface.

Add Vegetables and Seasonings:
- After simmering the chicken, add the chopped onions, minced garlic, diced carrots, diced potatoes, chopped celery, green peas, corn kernels, and bay leaf to the pot.
- Season with salt and pepper to taste.

Continue Cooking:
- Cover the pot and simmer the soup for another 30-40 minutes, or until the chicken is cooked through and the vegetables are tender.
- Adjust the seasoning with more salt and pepper if needed.

Serve:
- Once the soup is ready, remove the chicken pieces from the pot and shred the meat using forks. Discard the bones and skin.
- Return the shredded chicken meat to the pot and stir to combine.

- Ladle the Sopa Leão Veloso into serving bowls. If desired, serve the soup over cooked rice or noodles.
- Garnish with freshly chopped parsley or cilantro before serving.

Enjoy your Sopa Leão Veloso!

This Brazilian chicken soup is delicious, comforting, and packed with nutritious vegetables and tender chicken. Serve it hot and enjoy its hearty flavors. It's perfect for warming up on chilly days or whenever you're craving a comforting bowl of soup.

Canjica Nordestina (Northeastern Brazilian Corn Pudding)

Ingredients:

- 2 cups dried white corn kernels (canjica or hominy)
- 1 liter (4 cups) water
- 1 can (400ml) coconut milk
- 1 cup granulated sugar
- 1 cinnamon stick
- 4 cloves
- Pinch of salt
- Grated coconut (optional, for garnish)
- Ground cinnamon (optional, for garnish)

Instructions:

Prepare the Corn Kernels:
- Rinse the dried white corn kernels (canjica or hominy) thoroughly under cold water.
- Soak the corn kernels in water overnight or for at least 8 hours to soften.

Cook the Corn Kernels:
- After soaking, drain the corn kernels and transfer them to a large pot.
- Add 1 liter (4 cups) of water to the pot along with the drained corn kernels.
- Bring the water to a boil over medium-high heat, then reduce the heat to low and simmer gently for about 1 to 1.5 hours, or until the corn kernels are tender. Stir occasionally and add more water if necessary to prevent sticking.

Add the Coconut Milk and Sugar:
- Once the corn kernels are tender, add the coconut milk, granulated sugar, cinnamon stick, cloves, and a pinch of salt to the pot.
- Stir well to combine and continue cooking over low heat for another 20-30 minutes, stirring occasionally, until the mixture thickens slightly and the flavors meld together.

Serve:
- Once the Canjica Nordestina is ready, remove the cinnamon stick and cloves and discard them.
- Serve the Canjica Nordestina warm or chilled in individual bowls.
- Optionally, garnish each serving with grated coconut and a sprinkle of ground cinnamon for extra flavor and presentation.

Enjoy your Canjica Nordestina!

This creamy and comforting Brazilian dessert is perfect for enjoying on its own or as part of a festive celebration. Its rich coconut flavor and aromatic spices make it a delightful treat for any occasion.

Arroz Doce (Brazilian Rice Pudding)

Ingredients:

- 1 cup white rice (long-grain or medium-grain)
- 4 cups milk (whole milk or coconut milk for a dairy-free option)
- 1 cup granulated sugar
- 1 cinnamon stick
- Pinch of salt
- Ground cinnamon, for garnish
- Optional: 1 teaspoon vanilla extract or 1 cinnamon stick (for extra flavor)

Instructions:

Rinse and Cook the Rice:
- Rinse the white rice under cold water until the water runs clear.
- In a medium-sized saucepan, combine the rinsed rice with 2 cups of milk and bring it to a boil over medium heat.
- Reduce the heat to low, cover the saucepan, and let the rice simmer gently for about 15-20 minutes, or until the rice is cooked and most of the milk has been absorbed. Stir occasionally to prevent sticking.

Add Sugar and Remaining Milk:
- Once the rice is cooked, add the granulated sugar, cinnamon stick, pinch of salt, and the remaining 2 cups of milk to the saucepan.
- If using vanilla extract, add it now for extra flavor.

Simmer and Stir:
- Stir well to combine all the ingredients, then let the mixture simmer over low heat, uncovered, stirring frequently to prevent sticking and to ensure the pudding cooks evenly.
- Cook the rice pudding for about 20-30 minutes, or until it reaches your desired consistency. The rice should be creamy and soft, and the mixture should have thickened.

Serve:
- Once the Arroz Doce is ready, remove the cinnamon stick (if using).
- Transfer the rice pudding to serving bowls or a serving dish.
- Optionally, sprinkle ground cinnamon on top of each serving for extra flavor and garnish.

Enjoy your Arroz Doce!

This creamy and comforting Brazilian rice pudding can be enjoyed warm or chilled. It's perfect for serving as a dessert or as a sweet snack any time of the day. It's also a popular treat during festive occasions and celebrations in Brazil.

Bauru (Brazilian Sandwich)

Ingredients:

- French bread (or a similar type of crusty bread), sliced lengthwise
- Roast beef slices (you can use deli-style roast beef)
- Mozzarella cheese slices (traditionally, the original recipe uses queijo prato, a Brazilian cheese similar to mozzarella, but mozzarella is a common substitute)
- Tomato slices
- Pickle slices
- Butter (optional, for spreading on the bread)

Instructions:

    Preheat a grill or sandwich press.
    Slice the French bread lengthwise and spread butter on the inside of each half (if desired).
    Layer the roast beef, mozzarella cheese, tomato slices, and pickle slices on one half of the bread.
    Place the other half of the bread on top to form a sandwich.
    Place the sandwich on the grill or sandwich press and cook until the bread is toasted and the cheese is melted, typically for about 5-7 minutes.
    Once the sandwich is heated through and the cheese is melted, remove it from the grill or press.
    Cut the sandwich into smaller pieces, if desired, and serve hot.

You can customize the Bauru sandwich to your liking by adding other ingredients such as mayonnaise, mustard, lettuce, or different types of cheese. It's a versatile and flavorful sandwich that's perfect for a quick lunch or snack.

Galinhada (Brazilian Chicken and Rice)

Ingredients:

- 1 whole chicken, cut into pieces (or you can use chicken thighs or drumsticks)
- 2 cups of rice
- 4 cups of chicken broth (you can use store-bought or homemade)
- 1 onion, chopped
- 2 cloves of garlic, minced
- 2 tomatoes, diced
- 1 bell pepper, diced
- 1 carrot, diced
- 1/2 cup of green peas (fresh or frozen)
- 1/4 cup of chopped fresh parsley
- 2 tablespoons of vegetable oil
- Salt and pepper to taste
- Optional: 1 bay leaf, 1 teaspoon of paprika, 1/2 teaspoon of turmeric

Instructions:

In a large pot or Dutch oven, heat the vegetable oil over medium heat. Add the chopped onion and minced garlic, and sauté until they become soft and translucent.

Add the chicken pieces to the pot and season them with salt, pepper, paprika, and turmeric (if using). Cook the chicken until it is browned on all sides.

Once the chicken is browned, add the diced tomatoes, bell pepper, and carrot to the pot. Stir well to combine.

Pour the chicken broth into the pot, along with the rice and bay leaf (if using). Bring the mixture to a simmer.

Cover the pot with a lid and let the Galinhada cook over low heat for about 20-25 minutes, or until the rice is cooked and the chicken is tender. Stir occasionally to prevent the rice from sticking to the bottom of the pot.

About halfway through the cooking time, add the green peas to the pot and continue cooking until they are heated through.

Once the rice is cooked and the chicken is tender, remove the pot from the heat. Taste and adjust the seasoning if necessary.

Sprinkle chopped fresh parsley over the Galinhada before serving.

Serve the Galinhada hot, either on its own or accompanied by a salad or cooked vegetables.

Galinhada is a delicious and satisfying one-pot meal that's perfect for feeding a crowd or for a cozy family dinner. Feel free to customize the recipe by adding other vegetables or herbs according to your preference.

Casquinha de Siri (Stuffed Crab Shells)

Ingredients:

- 4-6 large crab shells (cleaned and prepared)
- 300g of fresh crab meat (you can also use canned crab meat)
- 1 onion, finely chopped
- 2 cloves of garlic, minced
- 1 tomato, diced
- 1/2 bell pepper, diced
- 1 tablespoon of olive oil
- 1 tablespoon of butter
- 1/4 cup of coconut milk (optional)
- 1/4 cup of breadcrumbs
- 1/4 cup of grated Parmesan cheese
- 1 tablespoon of chopped fresh parsley
- Juice of 1 lime or lemon
- Salt and pepper to taste
- Hot sauce (optional, for added spice)

Instructions:

Preheat your oven to 350°F (175°C).

In a skillet, heat the olive oil and butter over medium heat. Add the chopped onion and minced garlic, and sauté until they become soft and translucent.

Add the diced tomato and bell pepper to the skillet, and cook until they begin to soften.

Stir in the crab meat and coconut milk (if using) into the skillet. Cook for a few minutes until the crab meat is heated through and well combined with the other ingredients.

Season the mixture with salt, pepper, and hot sauce (if desired). Squeeze the lime or lemon juice over the mixture and stir well.

Remove the skillet from the heat and stir in the breadcrumbs, grated Parmesan cheese, and chopped parsley. Mix until everything is evenly combined.

Spoon the crab mixture into the cleaned crab shells, filling them up to the top.

Place the stuffed crab shells on a baking sheet and bake in the preheated oven for about 15-20 minutes, or until the tops are golden brown and the filling is heated through.

Once cooked, remove the stuffed crab shells from the oven and let them cool slightly before serving.
Serve the Casquinha de Siri hot as an appetizer or snack, garnished with additional chopped parsley and lime or lemon wedges if desired.

Casquinha de Siri is best enjoyed fresh out of the oven, with its creamy and savory filling complementing the natural sweetness of the crab meat. It's a delightful dish that showcases the flavors of the sea and is sure to impress your guests at any gathering.

Pastel de Nata (Portuguese Custard Tart)

Ingredients:

For the pastry:

- 1 sheet of puff pastry (store-bought or homemade)
- Flour, for dusting

For the custard filling:

- 2 cups of whole milk
- 6 large egg yolks
- 1/2 cup of granulated sugar
- 2 tablespoons of all-purpose flour
- 1 teaspoon of vanilla extract
- Zest of 1 lemon
- Cinnamon powder (optional, for garnish)

Instructions:

Preheat your oven to 475°F (245°C). Grease a muffin tin or tart molds with butter or non-stick cooking spray.

On a lightly floured surface, roll out the puff pastry sheet to about 1/8 inch thickness. Using a round cutter or glass, cut out circles slightly larger than the size of your tart molds.

Press each pastry circle into the prepared tart molds, making sure to cover the bottom and sides evenly. Trim any excess pastry if necessary.

In a saucepan, heat the milk over medium heat until it comes to a simmer. Remove from heat and set aside.

In a mixing bowl, whisk together the egg yolks, sugar, flour, vanilla extract, and lemon zest until smooth and well combined.

Slowly pour the hot milk into the egg mixture, whisking continuously to prevent the eggs from scrambling.

Once the mixture is well combined, pour it back into the saucepan and return to the heat. Cook over medium heat, stirring constantly, until the custard thickens and coats the back of a spoon, about 5-7 minutes. Remove from heat and let the custard cool slightly.

Spoon the custard into the prepared pastry shells, filling them about 3/4 full.

Place the filled tarts in the preheated oven and bake for 10-15 minutes, or until the pastry is golden brown and the custard is set with a slight jiggle in the center.

Remove the tarts from the oven and let them cool in the tart molds for a few minutes before transferring to a wire rack to cool completely.

Once cooled, sprinkle the Pastel de Nata with cinnamon powder, if desired.

Serve the Pastel de Nata warm or at room temperature, and enjoy these delightful Portuguese custard tarts as a sweet treat with a cup of coffee or tea.

These homemade Pastel de Nata are sure to impress with their flaky pastry and creamy custard filling, reminiscent of the authentic tarts found in Portuguese bakeries.

Sorvete de Creme com Calda de Goiabada (Cream Ice Cream with Guava Sauce)

Ingredients:

For the vanilla ice cream:

- 2 cups heavy cream
- 1 cup whole milk
- 3/4 cup granulated sugar
- 1 vanilla bean or 1 tablespoon vanilla extract
- Pinch of salt

For the guava sauce:

- 1 cup guava paste or guava jelly
- 1/2 cup water
- Juice of 1 lime or lemon
- Optional: 1 cinnamon stick

Instructions:

> To make the vanilla ice cream, start by preparing an ice bath. Fill a large bowl with ice water and set aside.
> In a saucepan, combine the heavy cream, whole milk, granulated sugar, and salt. If using a vanilla bean, split it open lengthwise and scrape the seeds into the saucepan, then add the vanilla bean pod as well. If using vanilla extract, add it to the mixture.
> Heat the mixture over medium heat, stirring occasionally, until it begins to steam but is not boiling. Remove from heat.
> If using a vanilla bean, remove the pod from the mixture. Allow the mixture to cool slightly, then transfer it to a bowl or container. Place the bowl/container in the ice bath to cool completely, stirring occasionally.
> Once the mixture is chilled, cover it and refrigerate for at least 4 hours or overnight.
> While the ice cream base is chilling, prepare the guava sauce. In a small saucepan, combine the guava paste or jelly with water, lime or lemon juice, and optional cinnamon stick. Heat over medium-low heat, stirring frequently, until the

guava paste/jelly has melted and the mixture has thickened slightly. Remove from heat and let it cool.

Once the ice cream base is chilled, churn it in an ice cream maker according to the manufacturer's instructions until it reaches a soft-serve consistency.

Transfer the churned ice cream to a freezer-safe container and freeze for at least 4 hours or until firm.

To serve, scoop the vanilla ice cream into bowls or cones and drizzle with the guava sauce.

Enjoy your Sorvete de Creme com Calda de Goiabada, savoring the creamy texture of the ice cream along with the sweet and tangy flavor of the guava sauce.

This dessert is a wonderful combination of flavors and textures, sure to delight your taste buds with its tropical flair.

Xinxim de Galinha (Chicken and Shrimp Stew)

Ingredients:

For the marinade:

- 2 lbs (about 1 kg) boneless, skinless chicken thighs, cut into bite-sized pieces
- Juice of 2-3 limes
- Salt and pepper to taste

For the stew:

- 1 lb (about 500g) large shrimp, peeled and deveined
- 2 tablespoons dendê oil (palm oil)
- 1 onion, finely chopped
- 3 cloves garlic, minced
- 1 red bell pepper, chopped
- 1 green bell pepper, chopped
- 1 cup unsalted peanuts, toasted and finely ground
- 1 cup coconut milk
- 2 tomatoes, chopped
- 1 tablespoon tomato paste
- 1 tablespoon ground coriander
- 1 tablespoon ground cumin
- 1 tablespoon paprika
- 1 tablespoon turmeric
- Salt and pepper to taste
- Chopped fresh cilantro or parsley for garnish
- Cooked rice, for serving

Instructions:

Marinate the chicken: In a bowl, combine the chicken pieces with lime juice, salt, and pepper. Let it marinate for at least 30 minutes, preferably longer in the refrigerator.

Heat the dendê oil in a large, deep skillet or Dutch oven over medium heat. Add the chopped onion and sauté until it becomes translucent.

Add the minced garlic, chopped bell peppers, and chopped tomatoes to the skillet. Cook until the vegetables soften.

Stir in the tomato paste, ground coriander, cumin, paprika, turmeric, salt, and pepper. Cook for another couple of minutes, allowing the spices to become fragrant.

Add the marinated chicken pieces to the skillet, stirring well to coat them with the spices. Cook until the chicken is no longer pink on the outside.

Pour in the coconut milk and bring the mixture to a simmer. Cover the skillet and let it simmer for about 20-25 minutes, or until the chicken is cooked through and tender.

Meanwhile, in a separate skillet, cook the peeled and deveined shrimp until they turn pink and opaque, about 2-3 minutes per side. Set aside.

Once the chicken is cooked, stir in the ground peanuts, followed by the cooked shrimp. Allow the stew to simmer for an additional 5 minutes to allow the flavors to meld together.

Taste and adjust the seasoning if necessary. If the stew is too thick, you can add a little water or more coconut milk to reach your desired consistency.

Garnish the Xinxim de Galinha with chopped fresh cilantro or parsley before serving.

Serve the stew hot over cooked rice, accompanied by additional lime wedges if desired.

Xinxim de Galinha is a comforting and aromatic dish that combines the flavors of Brazil's northeastern cuisine. It's perfect for sharing with friends and family, especially when served with rice to soak up all the delicious sauce. Enjoy!

Sarapatel (Pork Offal Stew)

Ingredients:

- 1 lb (about 500g) pork liver, cleaned and diced
- 1 lb (about 500g) pork heart, cleaned and diced
- 1 lb (about 500g) pork lungs, cleaned and diced
- 2 onions, finely chopped
- 4 cloves garlic, minced
- 2 tomatoes, diced
- 2 bay leaves
- 1 tablespoon paprika
- 1 tablespoon ground cumin
- 1 tablespoon ground coriander
- 1 tablespoon white vinegar
- Salt and pepper to taste
- Water or pork broth, as needed
- 1/4 cup dendê oil (palm oil)
- Chopped fresh cilantro or parsley for garnish
- Cooked rice, for serving

Instructions:

Start by preparing the pork offal. Clean the liver, heart, and lungs thoroughly under cold water. Remove any excess fat, membranes, or tough connective tissues. Dice the offal into small pieces and set aside.

In a large pot or Dutch oven, heat the dendê oil over medium heat. Add the chopped onions and minced garlic, and sauté until they become soft and translucent.

Add the diced tomatoes to the pot and cook until they start to break down and release their juices.

Stir in the diced pork offal (liver, heart, and lungs) into the pot, along with the bay leaves, paprika, ground cumin, ground coriander, white vinegar, salt, and pepper. Mix well to coat the offal with the spices.

Pour enough water or pork broth into the pot to cover the ingredients. Bring the mixture to a simmer.

Once the stew is simmering, reduce the heat to low and cover the pot. Let the Sarapatel cook for about 1 to 1.5 hours, stirring occasionally, or until the pork offal is tender and the flavors have melded together.

Taste and adjust the seasoning if necessary. If the stew is too thick, you can add more water or broth to reach your desired consistency.
Once the Sarapatel is cooked and tender, remove the bay leaves from the pot.
Garnish with chopped fresh cilantro or parsley before serving.
Serve the Sarapatel hot over cooked rice, accompanied by slices of toasted bread or farofa (toasted cassava flour) on the side.

Sarapatel is a rich and comforting dish with a unique flavor profile that comes from the combination of pork offal and aromatic spices. It's a beloved part of northeastern Brazilian cuisine and is often enjoyed during festive occasions and celebrations. Enjoy!

Rosquinhas de Coco (Coconut Cookies)

Ingredients:

- 2 cups shredded coconut (unsweetened)
- 1 cup all-purpose flour
- 1/2 cup granulated sugar
- 2 large eggs
- 1/4 cup unsalted butter, melted
- 1 teaspoon vanilla extract
- Pinch of salt
- Additional shredded coconut for coating (optional)

Instructions:

Preheat your oven to 350°F (175°C). Line a baking sheet with parchment paper or lightly grease it with butter or cooking spray.
In a mixing bowl, combine the shredded coconut, all-purpose flour, granulated sugar, and a pinch of salt. Mix well to combine.
In a separate bowl, beat the eggs lightly with a fork or whisk. Add the melted butter and vanilla extract to the beaten eggs and mix until well combined.
Pour the wet ingredients into the bowl of dry ingredients. Stir everything together until a dough forms. The dough will be slightly sticky.
Using your hands or a cookie scoop, shape the dough into small balls, about 1 inch in diameter. If desired, roll each ball of dough in additional shredded coconut to coat it.
Place the shaped cookies onto the prepared baking sheet, spacing them a couple of inches apart to allow for spreading.
Bake the Rosquinhas de Coco in the preheated oven for 12-15 minutes, or until the cookies are lightly golden brown around the edges.
Once baked, remove the cookies from the oven and let them cool on the baking sheet for a few minutes before transferring them to a wire rack to cool completely.
Once cooled, store the Rosquinhas de Coco in an airtight container at room temperature for up to a week.
Serve and enjoy these delicious coconut cookies as a snack or dessert.

These Rosquinhas de Coco are sure to be a hit with coconut lovers! They're simple to make and perfect for sharing with family and friends on any occasion.

Ambrosia (Brazilian Custard)

Ingredients:

- 4 cups whole milk
- 1 cup granulated sugar
- 4 large eggs
- Zest of 1 orange or lemon (optional)
- Cinnamon sticks or ground cinnamon for garnish (optional)
- Grated coconut for garnish (optional)

Instructions:

In a large saucepan, combine the whole milk and granulated sugar. Place the saucepan over medium heat and stir until the sugar is dissolved and the milk is warm.

In a separate bowl, beat the eggs until well combined. If using citrus zest, you can add it to the beaten eggs for additional flavor.

Gradually pour the beaten eggs into the warm milk mixture, stirring constantly to prevent the eggs from curdling.

Continue cooking the mixture over medium-low heat, stirring frequently, until it thickens to a custard-like consistency. This process may take about 20-30 minutes.

Once the Ambrosia has thickened, remove it from the heat and let it cool slightly. Transfer the Ambrosia to serving bowls or a large serving dish. Cover the surface with plastic wrap or parchment paper to prevent a skin from forming, and refrigerate until chilled.

Before serving, garnish the Ambrosia with cinnamon sticks or ground cinnamon for a hint of spice, and grated coconut for additional flavor and texture.

Serve the Ambrosia chilled as a refreshing dessert, especially on warm days or after a hearty meal.

Ambrosia is a comforting and delicious dessert that's loved by many in Brazil. Its creamy texture and subtle citrus flavor make it a delightful treat for any occasion. Feel free to adjust the sweetness or add your own twist with different garnishes to suit your taste preferences.

Caruru (Okra Stew)

Ingredients:

- 1 lb (about 500g) okra, washed, trimmed, and sliced
- 1 onion, finely chopped
- 2 cloves garlic, minced
- 2 tomatoes, diced
- 1/2 cup dried shrimp, soaked in water and drained
- 1/2 lb (about 250g) small shrimp, peeled and deveined
- 2 tablespoons dendê oil (palm oil)
- 1 tablespoon olive oil
- 1 tablespoon ground dried shrimp (optional, for extra flavor)
- 1 tablespoon ground coriander
- 1 tablespoon ground cumin
- 1 tablespoon ground paprika
- Salt and pepper to taste
- Chopped fresh cilantro or parsley for garnish
- Cooked white rice, for serving

Instructions:

Heat the dendê oil and olive oil in a large skillet or pot over medium heat.
Add the chopped onion and minced garlic to the skillet. Sauté until the onions are soft and translucent.
Add the diced tomatoes to the skillet and cook until they start to break down and release their juices.
Stir in the sliced okra and dried shrimp (both soaked and ground, if using). Cook for a few minutes until the okra begins to soften.
Add the ground coriander, cumin, paprika, salt, and pepper to the skillet. Mix well to coat the ingredients with the spices.
Pour in a small amount of water to the skillet, just enough to barely cover the ingredients. Cover the skillet and let the mixture simmer for about 10-15 minutes, or until the okra is tender.
Once the okra is tender, add the small shrimp to the skillet. Cook for an additional 3-5 minutes, or until the shrimp are pink and cooked through.
Taste and adjust the seasoning if necessary.
Serve the Caruru hot, garnished with chopped fresh cilantro or parsley.

Serve the Caruru as a side dish with cooked white rice.

Caruru is a delicious and nutritious dish with a unique flavor profile that showcases the vibrant and diverse cuisine of Brazil. Enjoy this flavorful okra stew as part of a traditional Brazilian meal or on its own as a satisfying and comforting dish.

Salada de Palmito (Hearts of Palm Salad)

Ingredients:

- 1 can (14 ounces) hearts of palm, drained and sliced
- 1 large tomato, diced
- 1/2 red onion, thinly sliced
- 1/4 cup chopped fresh parsley or cilantro
- Juice of 1 lime or lemon
- 2 tablespoons extra virgin olive oil
- Salt and pepper to taste
- Optional: sliced olives, diced bell peppers, avocado slices, shredded carrots, or other vegetables of your choice for additional flavor and texture

Instructions:

In a large salad bowl, combine the sliced hearts of palm, diced tomato, thinly sliced red onion, and chopped fresh parsley or cilantro.

In a small bowl, whisk together the lime or lemon juice and extra virgin olive oil to make the dressing. Season with salt and pepper to taste.

Pour the dressing over the salad ingredients in the bowl. Toss gently to coat everything evenly with the dressing.

If desired, add any optional ingredients such as sliced olives, diced bell peppers, avocado slices, or shredded carrots to the salad.

Taste the salad and adjust the seasoning if necessary, adding more salt, pepper, or citrus juice as desired.

Serve the Salada de Palmito immediately as a side dish or appetizer, or refrigerate it for about 30 minutes to allow the flavors to meld together before serving.

Enjoy this refreshing and nutritious Hearts of Palm Salad on its own or alongside grilled meats, seafood, or other Brazilian dishes.

Salada de Palmito is a versatile salad that can be customized to suit your taste preferences. Feel free to add or omit ingredients according to what you have on hand or your personal preferences. It's a perfect dish for warm weather gatherings or as a light and healthy addition to any meal.

Sururu com Leite de Coco (Clams in Coconut Milk)

Ingredients:

- 2 lbs (about 1 kg) fresh sururu (small clams), cleaned and scrubbed
- 1 can (14 ounces) coconut milk
- 1 onion, finely chopped
- 2 cloves garlic, minced
- 1 red bell pepper, diced
- 1 green bell pepper, diced
- 2 tomatoes, diced
- 1/2 cup chopped cilantro or parsley
- 2 tablespoons dendê oil (palm oil)
- 1 tablespoon olive oil
- Juice of 1 lime or lemon
- Salt and pepper to taste
- Optional: sliced green onions for garnish
- Cooked rice or crusty bread, for serving

Instructions:

In a large bowl, soak the cleaned sururu in cold water with a little bit of salt for about 30 minutes to an hour. This helps to remove any sand or grit from the clams.

After soaking, drain the sururu and rinse them thoroughly under cold water. Set aside.

In a large skillet or pot, heat the dendê oil and olive oil over medium heat.

Add the chopped onion and minced garlic to the skillet. Sauté until the onions are soft and translucent.

Stir in the diced red and green bell peppers, and cook for a few minutes until they start to soften.

Add the diced tomatoes to the skillet and cook until they begin to break down and release their juices.

Pour in the coconut milk and bring the mixture to a simmer.

Once the coconut milk is simmering, add the cleaned sururu to the skillet. Cover and cook for about 5-7 minutes, or until the clams have opened and are cooked through. Discard any clams that do not open.

Stir in the chopped cilantro or parsley and lime or lemon juice. Season with salt and pepper to taste.

Once the Sururu com Leite de Coco is cooked and seasoned to your liking, remove it from the heat.

Serve the Sururu com Leite de Coco hot, garnished with sliced green onions if desired, and accompanied by cooked rice or crusty bread.

Sururu com Leite de Coco is a delicious and aromatic seafood dish with a rich and creamy coconut milk broth. It's perfect for seafood lovers and makes for a satisfying meal, especially when served with rice or bread to soak up the flavorful broth. Enjoy!

Cocada Preta (Black Coconut Candy)

Ingredients:

- 2 cups shredded coconut (fresh or desiccated)
- 1 cup dark brown sugar
- 1/2 cup molasses or dark syrup (such as cane syrup or corn syrup)
- 1/4 cup water
- 1/4 teaspoon ground cinnamon (optional)
- Pinch of salt

Instructions:

In a large skillet or saucepan, combine the dark brown sugar, molasses or dark syrup, water, ground cinnamon (if using), and a pinch of salt. Stir well to combine. Place the skillet or saucepan over medium heat and bring the mixture to a gentle boil, stirring constantly.

Once the mixture is boiling, reduce the heat to low and add the shredded coconut. Stir well to coat the coconut evenly with the sugar syrup.

Continue cooking the mixture over low heat, stirring frequently, until it thickens and becomes glossy, and the coconut is well coated, about 10-15 minutes.

As the mixture cooks, it will darken in color. Keep a close eye on it to prevent burning, and adjust the heat as needed.

Once the Cocada mixture has thickened to your desired consistency and the coconut is evenly coated, remove it from the heat.

Allow the Cocada mixture to cool slightly until it is safe to handle.

While the mixture is still warm, shape it into small rounds or squares by pressing it firmly together with your hands. You can also use a spoon or small cookie scoop to portion out the Cocada onto a parchment-lined baking sheet.

Let the Cocada rounds or squares cool completely at room temperature until they are firm and set.

Once cooled and set, store the Cocada Preta in an airtight container at room temperature. It will keep well for several days.

Cocada Preta is a delicious and indulgent sweet treat with a rich, caramelized flavor and chewy texture. It's perfect for satisfying your sweet tooth and makes a delightful homemade gift or party favor. Enjoy!

Pamonha (Sweet Corn Tamale)

Ingredients:

- 6 ears of fresh corn, husks removed and kernels cut off the cob
- 1 cup granulated sugar (adjust to taste)
- 1/2 cup coconut milk (optional)
- Pinch of salt
- Corn husks, soaked in water for at least 30 minutes

Instructions:

In a blender or food processor, blend the corn kernels until they are finely ground but still slightly chunky.

Transfer the blended corn to a large bowl. Add the granulated sugar, coconut milk (if using), and a pinch of salt. Mix well to combine.

Take a soaked corn husk and lay it flat on a clean surface. Place about 1/4 to 1/3 cup of the corn mixture onto the center of the husk.

Fold the sides of the husk over the filling to enclose it, then fold the bottom of the husk up to seal the bottom. You can tie the husk closed with kitchen twine if desired.

Repeat the process with the remaining corn mixture and corn husks.

Fill a large pot with a few inches of water and place a steamer basket or rack inside. Arrange the pamonhas in the steamer basket, making sure they are not overcrowded.

Cover the pot with a lid and steam the pamonhas over medium heat for about 45-60 minutes, or until they are firm and cooked through.

Once cooked, remove the pamonhas from the steamer and let them cool slightly before serving.

Serve the pamonhas warm or at room temperature, either as a dessert or snack.

Pamonha is a delightful treat that showcases the natural sweetness of fresh corn. It's soft, creamy, and comforting, perfect for enjoying on its own or with a cup of coffee or tea. You can also experiment with adding other flavors such as cinnamon or cheese for variation. Enjoy!

Creme de Papaya com Cassis (Papaya Cream with Cassis Liqueur)

Ingredients:

- 1 ripe papaya, peeled, seeded, and diced
- 2 cups vanilla ice cream or heavy cream
- 2-4 tablespoons cassis liqueur (adjust to taste)
- Ice cubes (optional)
- Fresh mint leaves for garnish (optional)

Instructions:

Place the diced papaya and vanilla ice cream or heavy cream in a blender.
Blend the mixture until smooth and creamy. If the mixture is too thick, you can add a splash of milk or water to help it blend more easily.
Taste the papaya cream and adjust the sweetness if necessary by adding a little sugar or honey, if desired.
If you prefer a colder dessert, you can add a few ice cubes to the blender and blend until they are completely incorporated.
Once the papaya cream is smooth and creamy, divide it into serving glasses or bowls.
Drizzle 1-2 tablespoons of cassis liqueur over each serving of papaya cream.
Garnish the Creme de Papaya com Cassis with fresh mint leaves, if desired, for a pop of color and freshness.
Serve the dessert immediately, while it's still cold and refreshing.

Creme de Papaya com Cassis is a delightful dessert that's perfect for hot summer days or as a sweet ending to any meal. The creamy texture of the papaya combined with the sweet and tangy flavor of the cassis liqueur creates a wonderful contrast of flavors and textures. Enjoy this Brazilian treat with friends and family!

Mingau de Milho Verde (Brazilian Green Corn Porridge)

Ingredients:

- 4 ears of fresh green corn (corn on the cob)
- 2 cups milk (you can use whole milk or coconut milk for extra richness)
- 1/2 cup granulated sugar (adjust to taste)
- Pinch of salt
- Ground cinnamon or nutmeg for garnish (optional)

Instructions:

Remove the kernels from the ears of green corn. You can do this by holding each ear upright on a cutting board and using a sharp knife to slice down the sides of the cob to remove the kernels.

Place the green corn kernels in a blender or food processor. Add 1 cup of milk to the blender and blend until the mixture is smooth.

Strain the blended mixture through a fine mesh sieve or cheesecloth to remove any fibrous pieces. This will help ensure a smooth and creamy texture for the porridge.

In a saucepan, combine the strained corn mixture, remaining 1 cup of milk, granulated sugar, and a pinch of salt. Stir well to combine.

Place the saucepan over medium heat and bring the mixture to a simmer, stirring frequently to prevent sticking.

Once the mixture reaches a simmer, reduce the heat to low and let it cook, stirring occasionally, for about 10-15 minutes, or until it thickens to a creamy consistency.

Taste the Mingau de Milho Verde and adjust the sweetness if necessary by adding more sugar, if desired.

Once the porridge is cooked to your liking and has reached the desired consistency, remove it from the heat.

Serve the Mingau de Milho Verde warm in bowls, sprinkled with ground cinnamon or nutmeg for a warm and comforting flavor, if desired.

Mingau de Milho Verde is a delicious and comforting dish that highlights the natural sweetness of fresh green corn. It's perfect for enjoying as a breakfast or snack, especially on cooler days when you're craving something warm and satisfying. Feel free to customize the recipe by adding spices or additional flavorings to suit your taste preferences. Enjoy!

www.ingramcontent.com/pod-product-compliance
Lightning Source LLC
LaVergne TN
LVHW061946070526
838199LV00060B/3997